"Great book! It helps advisors to go beyond the words and the questions in the Values-Based Financial Planning™ and Financial Road Map® processes to create an experience for the prospect/client to really be heard. It gives us the simple changes we need to make to take our business to the next level. It gets down to hearing the true essence of the people we interact with and care about."

~ Jo Ellen Nevans, CFP,
Senior Financial Advisor, Nevans, Britt and Associates
(A financial advisory branch of American Express Financial Advisors)

"No wonder Bachrach is so revered in the financial planning industry. My first manager at IBM told me thirty-five years ago, 'You have two ears and one mouth. Use them in that proportion.' Bill takes it further and advises us to talk for five minutes and listen for fifty-five minutes. He has zeroed in on the human need to feel appreciated and listened to and shown financial advisors how to meet that need, to our own and our clients' advantage."

~ Alan Cranfield, B.A., R.F.P., CFP,
Assante Asset Management Ltd.

"Once again Bill Bachrach has created a powerful message in an easy-to-read and easy-to-apply format. Bill's advice over the past eight years has enhanced both my business and personal success. He has been one of the greatest influences in my career, and I am confident that when you implement what you read in this book, you too will grow professionally and personally."

~ Michael Lane, Director,
TIAA-CREF Advisor Services
Author, Secrets of the Wealth Makers

"Everyone who has been successful in our business knows the key is not so much what you say, but how you listen. If you apply the concepts in this book, I'm quite certain that you will enjoy even greater success both personally and professionally."

~ *John Lefferts, CLU, ChFC, CFP,*
President, AXA Advisors

"The book is unbelievable . . . Even though I have participated in the 3-Day Academy, the seminar program, and the Trusted Advisor Coach® program . . . this book drove home and emphasized so many human points. Learning to listen is taking me to another world, and the fruits will be more and deeper relationships. Thank you!"

~ *Jan T. Mohamed, CFP, AEP,*
King, Mohamed & Associates

"Amazing . . . I always thought I was a good listener, but after reading this book I realize I was just pretending to listen while waiting in silence for the opportunity to ask the next question. If you really care about your clients and your own success, you'll listen to what this book has to say. I believe that it is possible to grow one's business in markets like the current one. I've noticed that most people don't seek the help of a professional such as a doctor until there is some sort of pain, and current markets have caused pain for investors. They are seeking professionals to deal with this pain. You need to set yourself apart from the masses, and this book will help you accomplish just that."

~ *Keith D. Cline, Senior Vice-President,*
Investments, Raymond James and Associates

"This book couldn't have come at a better time! With the markets as tough as they are, only the best advisors will stay afloat. And listening is a critical skill for anyone committed to being at the top of this profession, during any kind of economic climate. This is a must-read for all advisors."

~ *Larry J. Rybka, JD, CFP, President and CEO,*
Valmark Securities, Inc.

"Bill has done it again! Bachrach has created a powerful process to help financial services professionals to focus on what is important — their clients — through listening well. It should be required reading for every financial advisor."

~ *John J. Bowen Jr., Founder and CEO,*
CEG Worldwide, LLC

"One of the most underdeveloped skills in the business world today is the skill of active listening — listening with the intent of truly understanding. In their new book, *It's All About Them: How Trusted Advisors Listen for Success,* Bill Bacharach and Steve Shapiro provide a concise, effective model for becoming a better and more empathetic listener. Mastery of the principles put forth in this book will make you more successful as an advisor and more effective as a person."

~ *Barry G. Knight, Senior Vice-President,*
Director of Sales Development and Training,
Pioneer Investments

"Powerful and insightful! On the road to Being Done,™ listening will ensure a successful journey."

~ *Al Haddad, CEO, Financial Profiles*

"Another home run! This book really takes what Bill teaches to an even higher level and helps clients and prospects have an even better experience when interacting with a trusted advisor. It helps us realize even more the importance of listening, and the impact it really has on all the people we interact with each day. I definitely plan on sharing this book with my peers."

~ Robert MacRae, CFP, RFP, CIM, Senior Financial Advisor,
Assante Capital Management, Ltd.

"This book is important because it addresses the neglected art of concentrating and really listening to what clients really mean and feel when they talk to advisors. Don't assume — read the book and you will improve your skills, knowledge and effectiveness."

~ John Newman, Group Sales Director
St. James's Place Capital

"Since converting my practice to Values-Based Financial Planning™ and the Being Done™ concept, I am more confident and comfortable in the way I do business. I'm now having so much fun! Bill's new book is a must-read. But don't just read it — actually implement it. It works!"

~ Hank Kochan, Jr.,
Main Street Management Company

"This is the best book for financial professionals ever written on the key skill of listening; it will double your income."

~ Brian Tracy, Author of Victory!

It's All About Them

How Trusted Advisors™
Listen for Success

BILL BACHRACH, CSP

and

STEVE SHAPIRO

First Edition 2002

Printed in the United States of America

ISBN 0-9623804-1-5

OTHER BOOKS BY BILL BACHRACH, CSP

*Values-Based Selling: The Art of Building High-Trust Client Relationships
for Financial Advisors, Insurance Agents and Investment Reps*

*High-Trust Leadership: A Proven System for Developing
an Organization of High-Performance Financial Professionals* (with Norman Levine)

Values-Based Financial Planning: The Art of Creating an Inspiring Financial Strategy

These and other resources available at www.BachrachVBS.com

OTHER BOOKS AND AUDIOS BY STEVE SHAPIRO

Listening For Success (book)

Mental Muscle — Seven Principles for Strengthening Your Sales (6-cassette audio program)

The Miracle of Listening (two-cassette audio program)

Steve Shapiro Live (CD)

Available at www.steveshapiro.com

TRADEMARKED WORDS

The following terms in this book are trademarked or registered marks
held by Bachrach & Associates, Inc.:
Being Done™ Study Group, Financial Road Map,® Trusted Advisor,™
Trusted Advisor Coach,® Values-Based Financial Planning,™
Values-Based Selling,™ Values Conversation™

Multi-Level Listening™ is a term trademarked by Steve Shapiro.

Chica Publications

DEDICATION

To the graduates of the Trusted Advisor™ Coach program
and the Values-Based Selling™ Academy.

You taught me so much with your openness and courage
to audiotape and videotape your interviews
so we could watch them, listen, and learn.
These ideas would not exist otherwise.

For me, it's all about you.

~ Bill Bachrach

Table of Contents

If You Listen to Them
They *Will* Listen to You

*"Give me the gift
of a listening heart."*
~ King Solomon

ISTENING IS LIKE PICKING FRUIT FROM A TREE.
Sometimes you get a rotten piece of fruit, sometimes it's mediocre,
and sometimes you get the juiciest, ripest piece. But you get to the good
fruit only by picking fruit. If you don't pick any, you don't get bad,
mediocre, *or* good fruit. Listening is like this. When you interrupt people,
finish their sentences, or talk so much they can't get a word in, it's like
cutting off a tree's branches before it's even had a chance to flower, let
alone bear fruit. But if you listen to people and try your best to learn
what they think is important, they will eventually produce ripe fruit for
you. Some of what they say may be irrelevant, incorrect, or misguided —
like rotten fruit. But some of it may give you the key to what motivates

and inspires them to take action. That's the ripe fruit you seek. In the course of a conversation when you're letting someone else talk, he or she may say, "I've been looking for a way to simplify my financial management for years." What nice, ripe fruit!

You won't even know this wonderful fruit is on the tree if you're talking too much or if you're not listening carefully. And you'll leave it hanging there if you don't know how to pick it. For example, let's say you're interviewing a prospective client for the first time. Many financial advisors would launch into talking all about their company and credentials, trying to make small talk, find common ground, build rapport, and search for a need to fill.

A better response, one that gets to the fruit, is to listen.

Especially on the first occasion you meet with people about their money, you want the conversation focused on them, not on you. At Bachrach & Associates, Inc., we've taught thousands of financial professionals how to conduct the most effective client interview. The first rule in using our Values Conversation™ is to precisely follow a two-step process for discovering whether a person is a potential fit with your practice.[1] This discovery happens in the first few minutes by 1) asking a set of key questions, and then 2) simply being quiet and *listening* to the person's responses.

Simple, yes, but easy? Apparently not. If listening were easy, or natural, everyone would do it. Listening takes discipline. Most advisors agree that

---

1. To learn more about the interview, see Bill Bachrach's *Values-Based Selling™: The Art of Building High-Trust Client Relationships for Financial Advisors, Insurance Agents, and Investment Reps* (Aim High Publishing, 1996), chapters 2–4.

we teach the best interview they've ever encountered, yet few get really good at implementing it. Why do some people produce huge results, and others don't? Typically, it's one of three things. Either they don't listen to what we taught them in the first place, or with good intentions they modify it and decrease the effectiveness, or they use what we teach but don't listen to their prospects and clients during the interview.

Everyone in the financial services business hears about the importance of listening, but how many really get good at it? No doubt you picked up this book because you know that if you were a better listener and listened more, you'd produce better results by getting better clients — in other words, the clients who are ideal for your business and who place all of their assets under your care. These ideal clients hire you to write plans, give you all their money, and ignore financial "pornography." Most important, when you advise them, they listen to you, which is evident when they take action on your advice. For that to happen, you must first listen to them and listen well.

This is a book that will help you refine that skill. It will not teach you what questions to ask or, worse, how to manipulate people or *pretend* you're listening so you can close the sale. Forget what you learned about listening from sales courses. Sales classes don't really teach you to listen; they teach you to pretend to listen so people will buy your stuff. This is a book about truly listening, because when you truly listen, your clients will buy everything you recommend without ever being sold.

We wrote this book primarily to help Bill's clients who use Values-Based Financial Planning™ and the Financial Road Map® interview. It draws in great part from what Bill has learned as the leader of his company's Trusted Advisor Coach® program, where assisting top producers has led him to take what he knows about listening to the next level. The combination of Steve's expertise in the general field of listening psychology, combined with Bill's unparalleled understanding of financial advisors in particular — both in and outside of his training programs — make us confident it will help you get better results, no matter what client acquisition methods you choose to implement.

- In Chapter 1, you will learn why listening will make you different, more powerful, better liked, and wiser.
- Chapter 2 will teach you what it really means to listen and how listening opens the door to human motivation.
- Chapter 3 will show you why listening is so important and why it's the most influential skill you possess.
- In chapter 4, you will learn what to listen for and pay attention to if you want to positively influence others. You'll also learn how to overcome the biggest waste of your precious time and tremendously increase your effectiveness.
- How to listen is the subject of chapter 5. You'll learn the simple, two-step formula and the advanced listening formula.
- Chapter 6 helps you see the big picture and put what you've learned into action today.

If you want to grow your business and realize your life's dreams, then read this book and practice what it preaches. You'll become a better listener and a better financial professional. Remembering it's all about them can help you move beyond being just a salesperson, broker, or gopher and propel you to being a coach or a mentor to your clients, what we call a Trusted Advisor.™

Chapter **1**

Give Clients
What They Really Want

*"Show up ready
to be no place else."*

~ Max Dixon

MOST OF US TEND TO LISTEN more to clients, colleagues, and bosses than to spouses, partners, and children. One report stated that fathers spend an average of seven minutes per week listening to their children. Spouses spend about twenty-six minutes per week in meaningful conversation with one another.

Yet this is hardly a compliment to our listening skills at work; it's simply a sad fact about our family relationships. Both personally and professionally, the people around us yearn for someone with the courage and the desire to listen. Everyone we meet feels a deep longing to be heard.

But who's listening?

We live in a society of talkers. We've learned to believe that the best talkers are the most influential leaders, top salespeople, and brightest personalities. Yet who attracts us most: people who talk a lot or people who listen well? Would you rather follow a leader who lectures or one who listens and responds to you? To whom would you rather entrust your financial future, a chatty salesperson or a Trusted Advisor™ who sincerely wants to know what's important to you? What would you like most from your spouse or partner? Your boss? We all yearn for someone to really listen to us.

Why? Renowned American psychologist William James observed, "The greatest need of the human soul is the need for appreciation, the need to feel important." When people listen to you, you know they care. When you listen to others, you show you care.

Paradoxically, when people know you care about them and their dreams, not just what you want from them, you tend to get what you want from them. In other words, you're more likely to get what you want from others when you focus on helping *them* get what *they* want. If you want people to put all of their assets in your hands, for example, then you had better focus on what it will do for them (e.g., simplify their lives, achieve their goals, fulfill their values), not what it will do for you.

Build Trust by Listening to Their Story, Not by Telling Yours

Last year, a company hired Bill to speak with its leaders who were in charge of helping employees make the transition from being insurance agents to financial planners. In preparation, they sent their training manual for review, and a quick read revealed the material hadn't quite caught up to the new aims of the company. The opening script:

> *Advisor.* This meeting is about me listening to you. One of the main things we're going to do in the meeting is really listen to you.

Off to a good start, right? You'd think so, except after this introduction there were seventeen pages of monologue! Assuming advisors said exactly what the script dictated, they would then talk for more than fifteen minutes solid, and potential clients would have to aggressively interrupt to be heard. The monologue included a description of the advisor's credentials, the company background, and the financial planning process, along with many little sales nuggets/bombs designed to "disturb," creating anxiety and fear. Next, the script suggested a transition.

Advisor. But, as I said earlier, we're here to listen to you.

Can you see the humor in this? The advisor was then directed to ask a question that would require at most a thirty-second answer. Another several minutes of "responding" to that answer with a scripted reply was supposed to create the illusion of listening.

The whole thing was laughable, as if people would feel they'd been heard simply because advisors said so. All that had been added to a typical sales pitch was the statement, "We're going to listen." This company had the idea that listening was important, but they didn't actually do it; in essence, they said, "I'm here to listen, and now I'm going to talk." That's not much different from being on your first date and saying to your potential sweetheart, "Now, dear, I want to hear all about you. But first, let me tell you . . . all about me!"

The company needed more than a speech to a few leaders to turn this problem around. Because they changed only the language about listening and not the behaviors, within months they realized they would never meet their objectives. So they retreated to selling insurance and cross-selling some investment products instead of becoming true financial planners. They did this despite overwhelming evidence that clients who have a true financial planner buy a lot more insurance and investments. Therefore, the client is better served, the advisor earns more money, and the company generates more revenue and profit.

Here's a scenario where saying you're going to listen can actually lead to listening. This is the introduction we teach at the Values-Based Selling™ Academy.

> *Advisor.* We're glad you came in to have this meeting today, because the fact that you two are here indicates you are sincere about making smart choices about your money. And we take that seriously, too.
>
> You'll notice we're going to take a lot of notes, and we're going to ask a lot of questions. We're audiotaping the meeting today because we want to have the opportunity to listen to this again before we give you any advice. Helping you make smart choices with your money is far too important for me to miss anything. You know how you can watch a movie a second or third time and see things you didn't see the first time through? *(Pause for response.)*
>
> Obviously, this is a lot more important than a movie. We want to have a permanent record of our conversation to refer to so we can do a better job for you.
>
> The first thing we're going to do is explore and listen to what's important to you . . .

The rest of the first meeting is an interview (notice we didn't say "presentation") with the advisor asking brief questions and letting the other people talk about their values, goals, and current financial reality as documented in the papers they brought with them to the first interview.

One of the most powerful exercises we teach advisors is to audiotape their interviews with prospective clients so they can hear the interview again. Why? To achieve two important objectives: Listening a second time helps advisors do a better job for their clients, and it also helps them to assess their listening skills. It might not surprise you to find out that although most advisors are willing to make the tape, some are reluctant to hear it. Evidently, people don't even like to listen to themselves!

Yet would it be reasonable to say that the client interview is to your success what the golf swing is to Tiger Woods' success? Realistically, most advisors will not achieve the level of excellence in their profession that Tiger has in golf, but surely they can learn from his amazing dedication to his sport. Probably the greatest golfer who ever lived, the man still videotapes his golf swing, examines it, and gets coaching to improve it all the time. He's constantly on that swing like dimples on a golf ball. Given his results, advisors would be wise to emulate his rigor in their own profession.

Many advisors send us videotapes for evaluation, much like Tiger sends his tapes to his coaches. We also receive audiotapes. In evaluating them, we use the 5/55 rule: If the interview lasts an hour, it should consist of five minutes of the advisor's voice (and after the introduction, every time we hear that voice, the sentence should end with a question mark) and fifty-five minutes of either the other person's voice or silence.

The exercise lets us capture and learn from existing habits. Again, who's talking more, the advisor or the potential client? How much time was spent on niceties and chitchat, versus how much time was invested in exploring what's important? Was the conversation natural or forced? Did the advisor try to "sell" financial services, or did he or she simply listen for a real fit, which is the basis of a high-trust relationship?

These tapes reveal that, in addition to talking too much in general, many people attempt to convey they're listening by filling silence with "Okay," or "Uh huh." They're working too hard to *appear* as if they're listening. But people who actually listen don't have to do anything to prove it. As we've said before, this isn't a book on how to act *as if* you're listening; this is a book on how to actually listen.

How about you? Even without a recording, you may already be aware of some of your own listening strengths and weaknesses. Are you listening to people? Or are you waiting for your turn to talk? Do you take the time to really understand their world, to see it through their eyes? Or do you look for someone to hear your story?

Are you committed enough to start taping your own interviews so you can get the most accurate answers to these questions? Perhaps you feel a bit reluctant and are concerned that clients will not want their interviews recorded. Here's the good news: People love it. Our advisor-clients report that they have been pleasantly surprised by their prospects' response to the recorder. It communicates a key message loud and clear: "I am not only going to pay attention to you during this interview, but I care enough about you that I am going to listen *again*, later, so I can be sure I heard you correctly and didn't miss anything important." It's all about them.

Advisors are, by definition, paid to give advice. Yet there may be times when all that's needed is for the advisor to simply listen so clients can vent. A good example is during a bad market when people receive statements with lots of red ink and market losses. Most people know there is nothing the advisor can do to change the past, and few clients actually blame their advisors for not being able to predict the future. They just need to express their dismay and feel the professional understands their personal distress. It's conceivable that many clients who leave advisors when markets tank do so not because they really believe another advisor will do a better job, but simply because they don't feel much empathy from the advisor they are leaving.

When a client vents, it presents a great time to introduce comprehensive planning — but only after you have listened thoroughly and well. On such an occasion, you can clearly serve your clients' best interests:

> *Advisor.* I hear your frustration with your investment performance. I am
> frustrated about it, too. That's one of the key reasons our firm is
> moving from investment planning to comprehensive financial
> planning. While we can't reverse the past, we believe that having a
> more comprehensive financial plan will provide you with the highest
> probability of achieving your goals, regardless of what happens in the
> market, the economy, or world events that are outside our control.

The bottom line? To become a Trusted Advisor,™ you must see how your business is not about you. When you're meeting someone new for the first time, it's not about you. When you're offering financial solutions, it's not about you. When you're guiding clients to implement the plan you write, it's not about you.

That's right: *It's all about them.* Therefore, you must listen for success.

If you consistently and progressively make a shift from talking less to listening more, you will experience a shift in your business and relationships that will astound you. So read on, and find out how to use your unique human ability to listen.

Chapter

2

Know the True Meaning
of Listening

"Listening is wanting to hear."
~ Jim Cathcart

ARL ROGERS, who was a great listener and one of the most influential psychologists in American history, founded the humanistic psychology movement and revolutionized psychotherapy with his concept of client-centered therapy. If you were to study his work, you would see that client-centered therapy, like a client-centered financial business, is all about listening. After thirty years of practice and research, Carl Rogers concluded that *listening is the greatest tool we have for releasing human potential in others.*

Listening opens the door to human motivation. You cannot motivate people to do something they don't want to do. The adage is true: "A person convinced against his will is of the same opinion still." You can force them to do it. You can coerce them to do it. You can pay them to do it. But when you quit forcing, coercing, or paying, it's all over. *You can't motivate people to do something they don't want to do.* Motivation dwells within. It is human nature to move away from things that hurt, from things that detract from the quality of life, and toward things that feel good and enhance life's experiences. When you find out what those things are, for individual people, you have the key to what motivates them.

You cannot find this out if you're talking. No matter how persuasive you are, you cannot convince others to do something they don't want to do. No matter how many good reasons you give them — financial freedom! early retirement! vacations! a legacy! — they are still *your* reasons, not *their* reasons.

Probably the greatest weakness among financial professionals is they talk too much. If you're talking, you're not learning anything. If you're talking, you can't acquire knowledge about other people. You can't know what they want, what they need, what's important to them, or why they want what they want. You can know only what's important to you. And when you're the one doing the talking, they get the message loud and clear about what's important to you, too. By talking too much, you tell them that what you really want is for them to buy your stuff so you can get paid.

What's more, all this chattering can actually drive away people who would otherwise be sincerely interested in doing business. We've known countless financial professionals who used to get so absorbed in doing their routine (educating, explaining, justifying) that they had to be taught when to shut up and just allow themselves to be hired. Many financially successful people (ideal clients) don't need or want to be educated about the numbers, why certain investments or insurance plans are selected by the Trusted Advisor,™ or any of the technical aspects of the financial plan. They just want to be told what they need to do so they can get on with their lives.

Your Real Goal: Look for Fit

Does this mean listening will enable you to change every person's mind from no to yes? Of course not, and that shouldn't even be your goal. What listening will do is give you your best chance to develop high-trust relationships. Yet some people will have closed minds, and that's all there is to it. Let them go. Don't waste your time or theirs. Others sit on the fence, unsure. They might convince themselves if they learn more — about themselves. Don't lose them by talking too much. You increase the odds of creating a high-trust relationship by approaching them with a listening heart. And the only way you can recognize a good fit between your business and the prospective client is to listen.

Just remember, listening is not . . .

- Giving advice, which should come only after you've listened a great deal
- Telling your story, your company story, or your investment philosophy
- Probing for hot buttons
- Asking loaded questions designed to disturb and create pain, discomfort, dissatisfaction, guilt, and so on
- Punctuating the conversation with "uh huh," "right," "go on," and other fillers
- Half-listening because good, kind, or nice people do
- Hanging in because you don't know how to get away without hurting or offending someone

- Pretending you're interested when you're not
- Looking for the weak points in an argument so you can always be right, gathering ammunition for attack
- Seeking one specific piece of information at the expense of everything else
- Preparing your next comment while the other person is talking
- Sitting still with your mouth shut (a corpse can do that)
- Being passive (listening is an active process)
- Waiting for your turn to talk

One of the best listeners we know is also deaf. Because he cannot hear with his ears, he must focus his full attention on the speaker's body language, facial expressions, and lips. He asks questions to gain clarity, and his responses come only after he carefully considers what the speaker has communicated.

Clearly, listening is not the same as hearing. Hearing is a physiological process. Listening is a mental and emotional process. In a recent conversation, speaker and author Jim Cathcart said, "Listening is *wanting* to hear." Author M. Scott Peck writes that he once listened so hard to understand a speaker that he began to sweat. Now, *that* is wanting to hear.

You may not need to sweat to listen well, but to apply the listening skills you learn in this book, you'll need to work at it and practice, practice, practice. We can guarantee you that the enormous payoff will make it worth the effort. With practice, listening will become natural to you. When people sense that it's all about them, they will be even more attracted to you. They will tell you what a great listener you are. You will be able to identify those people who can become your greatest clients. And they'll listen to you, too.

Chapter 3

Pay Attention and Earn Trust

*"Trust cannot be built
where judgement is present."*

~ Stuart Wells

OST OF US in the financial services industry have been taught that persistence (a.k.a. high-pressure sales) is our ticket to paradise, but Trusted Advisors™ know the high-trust relationship is the key. And two things kill trust faster than anything else does: pressuring people and judging them. To listen, you must suspend your judgment and allow yourself to be fully present with the other person.

Listening is the opposite of pressure, which is like a brake on the wheel of progress. Instead, listening is the fuel of progress in the financial services business. Listening leads to success.

Genuine listening makes genuine honesty possible. When people feel both respected and heard, they are more inclined to reveal themselves. As a Trusted Advisor,™ you want people to tell you the truth about their money and their objectives, and you also want people to be able to hear and act on the truth you will be communicating. Both ways, the truth has a lot of power.

Max Dixon, a well-known speaker, writer, and communication coach, is known for talking about creating a place for the "truth to descend." Listening is one of the factors in creating such a place. The nonverbal cues of attentive listening communicate volumes. According to Max, these are the most important messages:

- "I hear your story."
- "I understand and value your story."
- "You can trust me." ("I am trustworthy.")
- "I will never abandon you."
- "You are always welcome here."

It's your job to convey these messages without ever saying a word, to create a space where truths can be spoken, heard, and believed. Trust is the key to having all three, and listening is the building block of trust. Indeed, if you don't have trust, people won't be willing to tell you their truth or be able to listen to the truth you tell them.

If you don't have trust, you can tell people the truth, but they won't believe it. Think about the last time you answered the phone and the telemarketer calling you wanted to know about your phone bill so he or she could "save you a ton of money" on long distance. Since there was no trust, just pressure and probably an annoying interruption of dinner, you weren't willing to reveal your current long distance charges. You didn't want to hear how you could save money, and you didn't really believe it could be done, anyway. Maybe you really could have saved money by switching, but the building blocks of trust were absent, so you'll never know, and you don't care.

One of the cornerstones of your business is having clients implement the plan you create for them. Obviously, this is where the rubber meets the road, where clients make a commitment to their goals and to you as their financial advisor. Wouldn't you prefer a practice full of loyal clients who simply follow your advice? Again, it's all about creating a space where truths can be spoken, heard, and believed. When you tell people the truth about the plan you design for them, if they trust you, they will recognize how your plan will benefit them, and they will implement it. They may have a question or two, but resisting, objecting, or procrastinating would be the furthest things from their minds. After all, they want the results from implementing the plan more than you want to sell investments and insurance.

If your clients are not implementing, then back up a few steps and reexamine your listening skills. Maybe you didn't really hear what they had to say in your initial client interview. Maybe you didn't simply ask and listen; maybe you got caught up in telling your story. Did you find out what inspires them? What moves them? What motivates them every day? Was it clear from those discoveries how you could help them make decisions that will move them toward those things? Are they clear about how taking action right now will give them the highest probability of achieving their goals in a way that provides greater values fulfillment? Did you make it clear that you weren't there just to sell stuff and make commissions, but that for you, it's all about them?

You probably know from personal experience that not listening causes pain in your personal and professional relationships — conflicts, misunderstandings, arguments, lost business, and hurt feelings — much of which you can avoid by listening. *The quality of your relationships determines the quality of your life.* Poor quality relationships lead to a poor quality of life. High quality relationships lead to a high quality of life. Think about the most painful moments of your life; they probably involved some kind of conflict with another person. Remember the happiest moments of your life; they probably involved an experience of understanding or connection with another person.

People tend to listen least when they need to listen most. When the heat of emotion pushes your buttons and pulls your triggers, that is when you most need to listen. Unfortunately, it is also when listening becomes most difficult! Anger, frustration, and disappointment become "emotional cotton" in your ears.

When you stop to take a breath and bring yourself back to the present so you can hear what the other person is saying — when you take the cotton out of your ears — does that mean problems are automatically resolved? Of course not. What it means is that they have the *possibility* of getting resolved. Without listening, problems in human relations don't get solved. And they rarely just go away. They get stuffed or stowed. The feelings are buried, and feelings buried alive tend to live. Then they fester and grow like a cancer, killing intimacy, understanding, and joy.

Carl Rogers described the power of listening in his book, *On Becoming a Person*. He wrote,

> [Listening] is the most powerful force we know for altering the basic
> personality structure of an individual and improving his relationships
> and his communication with others. If I can listen to what he can tell
> me, if I can understand how it seems to him, if I can see its personal

meaning for him, if I can sense the emotional flavor it has for him,
then I will be releasing potent forces of change in him.

Here is an exercise Carl Rogers recommends if you want to do two things: improve your relationship with someone you care about and find out how hard it is to really listen.

The next time you get into an argument with someone, stop the discussion for a moment, and as an experiment, institute this rule: Each person can speak up only after he or she has first restated the ideas and feelings of the other speaker accurately, and to that speaker's satisfaction.

You will probably discover that this is one of the most difficult things you have ever tried to do. It takes *courage*, because to attempt to understand a person this deeply, to permit yourself to enter someone else's private world and try to see the way life appears to them, is to run the risk of being changed. And to most people, the risk of being changed is a truly frightening prospect.

But there is no growth without change. To change is to grow. If you want to grow personally and professionally, if you want to become more effective in your relationships, more effective at attracting and retaining ideal clients, then you must learn to listen a little bit better each day.

Chapter 4

Hear the Truth, Tell the Truth and Get the Truth Every Time

"Wisdom is the reward you get
for a lifetime of listening when
you'd rather have been talking."

~ Aristotle

ISTEN FOR THE MESSAGE behind the message. To listen effectively, you need to listen to more than the *presenting message*. The presenting message is communicated with words, but words are only part of communication. The real message often runs deeper, beneath the words.

When emotions are involved, most of the meaning in a person's message lies under the waterline. So listening only to the words is like seeing the tip of an iceberg and believing you've seen the whole thing. Ninety percent of the iceberg lies under the water and ninety percent of the meaning in communication lies hidden beneath the words.

You must listen to the space between the words. Effective listening requires you to understand the message behind the message. You listen not only to the *lyrics*, but also to the *music*. You listen not only for the *content* of the message, but also for the *intent* as well. This is why, in a client interview, you are silent instead of trying to fill the space with your own voice. In the silence, you are still listening.

Remember, before you can respond effectively, you need to get a handle on the message behind the message, what radio personality Paul Harvey calls "the rest of the story." When someone is angry, what's behind the anger? When someone is sad, where does the sadness come from? When someone is joyful, what's behind that emotion? Connecting with another person at this level is what human-potential author Ken Keyes calls "the instant consciousness doubler." When you attempt to see things from another person's point of view, you have doubled your consciousness because you now see twice as much as you did before.

Insight, not insistence, is the key to persuasion. You cannot persuade someone by insisting they see things your way. You need to listen until you see things their way. And you do that by asking questions and listening. Only then can you open the door to persuasion. *Before you can take people where you want them to go, you need to start where they are.* The best way to do this is to listen for the message behind the message.

When a potential client tells you, "I have multiple advisors because that's how I ensure diversification," what is really being said? Maybe the person truly believes this is the best way to diversify. If you have established trust, you can be blunt and know the truth will be heard and accepted: "Oh, c'mon, that's not true. Having multiple advisors simply complicates your life and multiplies the number of things that can be overlooked in your planning. Having one advisor simplifies things, and you can still have the all the diversification that is prudent for you."

But listen closely. Maybe the person doesn't really believe that line and is using it as an excuse to keep you at a distance. What the person is really saying is, "I don't trust you to handle all my money." If that's the message, then you'd better get some clarification and start dealing with the problem, either by improving your competence or improving your relationship. You'll know which one.

But yammering on, trying to convince someone, is a waste of your breath. Talking tends to push, and listening tends to pull. Pushing tends to create resistance, and pulling tends to create assistance. Trying to convince people by talking them into your way of seeing things is like pushing a red wagon by its black handle. The wagon goes every direction except the one you want it to go. Pull the wagon, and it follows. Insight, not insistence, overcomes resistance.

Listen for High-Trust Relationships

If you were to lead a team that must survive in the jungle without supplies for one month, and you got to choose who to bring, would you take along just anyone? Of course not. You would screen your potential team members carefully. After all, your life and theirs would depend on it.

Approach client acquisition the same way. Who is your ideal client? A precise definition of the kind of person you can best serve and who will be most advantageous to your financial practice makes all the difference in attracting, recognizing, and keeping ideal clients. Think about your best clients and consider what makes them so rewarding. Ask yourself how they're alike financially, professionally, or personally, and what attitudes and aptitudes set them apart. You must also ask yourself, "Is this someone I would enjoy talking to frequently? Do I trust this person?"

You know what it's like when you look at your calendar, see a certain person's name on your schedule, and think to yourself, "Oh, him. Bummer." And you also know what it's like to see an appointment on your calendar for a person with whom you want to spend time. Your ideal client is that second person. A detailed and specific profile is essential, and the following is an example. Notice how the profile reflects both the financial and psychological aspects of the person.

Ideal Client Profile
- Is serious about personal financial success
- Has goals and is motivated to achieve them
- Earns a total household income of at least $_____
- Is eager to send me everyone they know who fits my profile
- Is open minded
- Has investable assets of $_____
- Isn't influenced by financial media (ignores financial "pornography")
- Recognizes other things in life that are more important than money
- Enjoys life
- Is receptive to professional relationships and not a do-it-yourselfer; more of a financial delegator

If you could conduct business in a way that fulfills your desires to help people, to build a successful business, and to enjoy both the process and the result, wouldn't you want to do it? If so, here's our advice to you: Work only with those clients who "get it."

You know what we mean. Haven't you noticed that some people you meet just don't get it? They are content to go it alone, however much hassle that may entail. They are clueless about the benefits a relationship with you would bring. Even if you acted it out for them in a blockbuster presentation on Broadway, they *still wouldn't get it.* And haven't you noticed that some people, as soon as they hear the general gist of how a Trusted Advisor™ can change their lives, are ready to take action right now? Some people get it and some don't get it. One of the most important reasons to listen is to quickly distinguish between those who get it and those who don't.

At Bachrach & Associates, Inc., we provide our advisor-clients with a Financial Road Map,® an invaluable tool for both working with clients and screening prospects.[2] Think of it as an IQ test for the potential client. You help them explore and discover their values and put those in writing. You define and prioritize their most important goals in life, and you summarize their current financial truth all on one big, colorful, easy-to-understand piece of paper (the Financial Road Map®). Then you propose to write a comprehensive financial plan and offer to be their coach, their mentor, and their guide to implement that plan so they can actualize all they've expressed to you that they desire — in other words, you offer to give them the highest probability of getting everything they want for their reasons. If, after all that, they say anything other than yes, they have failed the test. *They don't get it.* By the time you reach that point, there should be no reason for stalling. Either they get it or they don't. People who get it hire you now.

---

2. To learn more about the Financial Road Map®, see Bill Bachrach's *Values-Based Selling: The Art of Building High-Trust Client Relationships for Financial Advisors, Insurance Agents, and Investment Reps* (Aim High Publishing, 1996), chapter 6, "Create a Financial Strategy Masterpiece."

Clearly, you want to build your business with people who get it. Perhaps you remember the lesson of the three little pigs: Build your house of solid materials, and no hungry wolf can take it down, no matter how hard he huffs and puffs. Likewise, build your business with the right kind of clients, and nothing can threaten the high-trust relationships that are the foundation of your success. This is the reason why some advisors sail through bear markets, recessions, and tragic world events. Not only do they retain clients during these times, but they also add more of exactly the kind of clients they want. It's true: During the very times when many advisors seriously consider quitting the business, struggle to find anyone remotely interested in becoming a client, or suffer significant financial reversals, Trusted Advisors™ who use our methods consistently attract more of the right kind of clients.

Beyond the "get it" and "don't get it" distinction, you can listen to categorize three types of people who seek financial planning. They are the do-it-yourselfers, the collaborators, and the delegators.

Do-it-yourselfers. By definition, do-it-yourselfers are not ideal clients for Trusted Advisors™: They are on their own because they don't want to work with anyone else. Some enjoy managing their own money and are capable of doing so. Some don't trust anybody to help them, so they have to do it themselves. Some just have their priorities mixed up and think that fiddling with their finances is more important than spending time with their families, exercising, educating themselves, or any of the other pursuits that are more meaningful to living a quality life than playing with money.

Trying to work with do-it-yourselfers is like building your house of straw. They make poor clients, primarily because they see more value in doing it themselves than in working with you, and it's hard to persuade them otherwise. Don't even try. Remember, your job is to listen for people who would naturally value and benefit from working with you, not to convince everyone how much they need you.

Collaborators. Just as a house made of wood is only slightly better than one of straw, so is a business built on collaborator-type clients only slightly better than one with do-it-yourselfers. Collaborators mostly want to do it themselves, but they want a relationship with an advisor so they'll have a gopher — or a scapegoat. They want you to educate them, do their research for them, and confirm their own research. "Is now a good time to buy gold?" they intone. "What's happening in the Asian markets, and how will that affect me?" Collaborators are merely do-it-yourselfers with an advisor in tow. They're in the driver's seat, and sooner or later they'll figure out that all the advisor does is give them confidence and information they could get for themselves. Once they realize this, they dump the advisor and become full-fledged do-it-yourselfers. When you work with collaborators, you are nothing more than a well-paid gopher, broker, agent, or salesperson. You certainly are not their advisor, mentor, or coach. Otherwise, they would follow your advice.

Delegators. Want to build a brick house? Find financial delegators. These are the people who get it, who want to tell you the truth so you can do your best for them, and who want to hear the truth because it leads to successful action on their part. They don't want to collaborate with you — they know comprehensive planning and implementation supervision are the key values you provide. They are happy to delegate their finances to you so they can focus on the things that are not only more important, but *cannot be delegated to anyone else* — things like being with their families, exploring their spirituality, improving their physical and mental health, being successful in their careers, and having more fun. These are people who value your advice. They respond to your coaching and value your financial mentoring.

Listening to people allows you to screen early and often. In traditional sales training, however, you are urged to take all comers then segment them later into A, B, and C categories, with As being the most likely to bring you profit and enjoyment (in our terms, an ideal client), and Cs being least likely to do so. Then you're supposed to focus on the As while still serving and making some money from the Bs and Cs, just in case.

But we suggest you think about it another way. Begin to see how recognizing the difference right away by listening more carefully, then serving only A clients — only ideal clients — should be your objective.

Gary Moore, a top producer with Merrill Lynch in Amarillo, has been in the business for twenty-two years and succeeded by most anyone's standards. It was just last year, however, when he realized how important it is for him to fill his practice with ideal clients so he can, in his words, "make sure that the second half of my life is a lot more fun than the first half, and I had a lot of fun in the first half." Bachrach & Associates, Inc. is now assisting him in driving toward this goal.

When Gary attended a seminar with about thirty other million-dollar producers at his company's training center in Princeton, New Jersey, one of the topics was segmenting the client base into groups of A, B, and C clients so advisors could spend most of their time with those clients who do the most business with them. Each advisor was telling the group his or her own method for such segmenting.

When it was Gary's turn, he responded, "Well, I'm striving to have only A clients."

The facilitator asked, "What do you do with the rest of them, Gary?"

Gary insisted, "I will not have any others. I'm going to have only A clients."

Later, Gary reported, "It was interesting that none of my colleagues had ever thought about that, and the folks that were putting on the training were . . . I don't want to say dumbfounded, but they were taken aback because they hadn't thought about it, either."

Gary needs this kind of focus to achieve his practice's objectives. Today he has only A clients and few exceptions, who are family and close friends. He can't allow any B or C clients because they just don't fit the business model. "This process is not all a bed of roses," he admits. "Some people I don't mind disengaging from, but others . . .". Yet he realizes that if he's going to build his practice the way he wants to, he's got to be honest with himself and his clients about whether there's a fit or not. He's just keeping his eyes on the prize because he knows this approach is what's best not only for him but, most important, what's best for his clients. Gary knows that as he's driving for success in his business, it's all about them.

This follows sound principles of business management. In Jim Collins' book, *Good to Great* (2001, HarperCollins), one of the executives he quotes reveals that to deliver to the people who are achieving, you can't be weighed down by those who are not. In our terms, you go from being a good to a great advisor by having only A clients. The only way to deliver to your A clients is to keep yourself and your staff unburdened with any B or C clients. Build an A-only clientele, as Gary has done.

What's more, clients would rather be one of a hundred rather than one of nine hundred or nineteen hundred you serve. Indeed, when financial advisor Brownie Sides told his clients he was transitioning from a transaction-oriented, marketing machine type of business to a full-service financial advisory practice, he was pleasantly surprised at how quickly some of his clients got it and realized it's all about them.

"Well, am I in?" many asked.

And some also inquired, "How do I get my friends in before the deadline?"[3]

Wow. Music to any advisor's ears, isn't it?

---

3. Both Gary and Brownie have participated in the Values-Based Selling™ Academy, Trusted Advisor® Coach program, and are now involved with the Being Done™ Study Group. For more information on this and other coaching support from Bachrach & Associates, Inc., see the back of this book, visit www.BachrachVBS.com, or call (800) 347-3707.

Chapter 5

Master the Two Steps of Listening for Success and Reap the Rewards

*"I think the one lesson I have
learned is that there is no
substitute for paying attention."*

~ Diane Sawyer

OLLOWING is the short model for effective listening.
Master it first, then move on to the advanced model. The short
model has two steps and it goes like this:

Ask! Listen!

That's it. Notice that *talk* is not in this formula. Most financial pros
use a different formula. It has two steps, also, but it goes like this:

Talk! Talk more!

We recommend the first model. Ask with enthusiasm and sincere
interest, then listen with great attention. Here's another way to look at
the two-step formula for listening:

Shut up, and pay attention!

It should be getting crystal clear why this is so important in creating high-trust relationships with your clients. It's also invaluable in your personal life. Where did people get the idea that it's their job to fix other people's problems? When did they begin to believe they had to have an answer to help their friends in pain, when all they really want and need is someone to listen and understand?

People don't want you to have a pat solution to their needs, not even as a financial advisor who is, by definition, supposed to provide advice. What makes the difference is listening first. If you were to supply an instant, unconsidered solution, you would completely discredit the seriousness of the issue, and you would therefore discredit the person who presented it.

Instead, you must listen first. You'll quickly discover how difficult this is to do, but you must form a new, better habit. It's like giving up cigarettes and replacing them with vitamins. Talking too much is to relationships what cigarettes are to the body, while listening is to your relationships what vitamins are to the body. One promotes disease, and the other promotes health.

So before going to the advanced model, the Multi-Level Listening™ model, you need to first master the two-step formula. Why? Because the law of listening says, "You gotta wanna." Just as there are clients who get it and those who don't, so are there advisors who get it and those who don't. And if you want to get it, to become an excellent listener for all the right reasons, the moral is, first, *you gotta wanna.*

The Multi-Level Listening™ Model

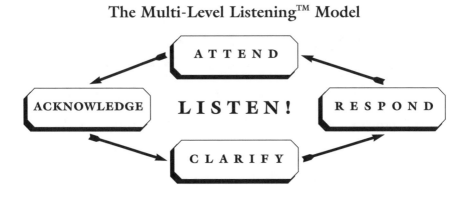

Paying Attention

The first key to effective listening is to attend. *Attend* means "to pay attention," and this is perhaps the most difficult step to effective listening, because the mind is so easily distracted. Paying attention takes practice.

Two types of distractions — external and internal — prevent you from paying attention to the speaker. External distractions include noises, other people, telephones, or something about the people you're listening to, such as the way they dress, or the way they talk. Internal distractions make it even more difficult. Thinking about other things, thinking about what you're going to say next, jumping to conclusions, mind reading, and making assumptions about the speaker's meaning, all get in the way of true communication.

This is one of the key reasons we teach advisors to have their first meeting with a prospective client at the advisor's office. Remember, it's all about them. It's not for the advisors' convenience or even, as some sales-people would say, for the clients' convenience; it's to maximize the clients' experience and minimize distractions for both of you. When they come to your office with all their documents and both spouses, you create a better environment for them. It's not possible for them to have created the perfect place for a successful financial meeting at their home or office. You, however, can set up the ideal space, an environment free from interruptions that creates the highest probability for them to express themselves freely and for you to really hear what they are saying, verbally and nonverbally.

The more you attend, the better you get at it. Attending also has a powerful effect on other people. They begin to open up and to share more of themselves. New levels of trust develop. It makes them feel important.

Do this one thing the next time someone talks to you: Make it all about them. Pay attention. Attend. Then attend some more. Practice and never stop practicing. You will get better, and it will transform your communication and your results.

Showing You've Paid Attention

The next key is to acknowledge. When you acknowledge what other people have said, you show concern and respect for them. You prove you are a responsive and caring person. Another word for acknowledge is *empathize.* You empathize with speakers, acknowledging their position. It doesn't mean you agree with them. It doesn't even mean you *understand* them. You are simply letting them know you have paid attention.

One of the things we talk about in the Trusted Advisor Coach® program is that you may never truly understand how another person feels. It may be impossible. When Bill watches his wife ride a horse on a wide-open plain in Montana, he can see that she is experiencing some form of nirvana. He knows she feels really good, but he will never perfectly understand how she feels — and he doesn't have to. All he has to do is contribute to her having more experiences like that and enjoy the knowledge that she is as close to heaven as she can be on earth.

Perfect understanding is not what really matters. What matters is that you listen so you can help people take appropriate action for their own reasons. This is especially true in the first interview. The purpose of the Values Conversation,™ which is the cornerstone in the first interview we teach, is not that the advisor understands the client's values. Again, it is all about them, the prospective clients. The purpose is that *they* have clarity about what's important to them so *they* can make better decisions. Roy Disney once said, "When your values are clear your decisions are easy." When your client understands what's important, and you know what your client considers important, you have succeeded.

There are many ways to acknowledge a speaker. One of the best is simply to *pause* when the speaker has finished. As a speaker yourself, you may have noticed that most "listeners" begin talking right away, sometimes before the last word has left your lips. And sometimes they interrupt you. What message does this send? It says they haven't listened to you. They've been formulating their response while you were talking. So if you want to acknowledge a speaker, just pause and look the person in the eye. Pause before you pick up the pen and record their answers. (That's right, the pen should not be in your hand while you are listening. It is a tool for writing, not a listening aid. When you have a pen in your hand and you ask a question, the client will feel pressure to answer, as though the *Jeopardy* music is playing in the background.) Pause for two to four seconds. Steve calls this the *Golden Silence*. What message does this send? It says, "What you've said is important enough for me to reflect upon before I respond. I have listened, and now I'm considering what you mean."

Pausing often feels uncomfortable at first. Most people aren't used to silence in communication. A great way to pause is simply to take a deep breath. It's impossible to talk and take a deep breath at the same time.

Remember, in communication it's the little things that make the big difference. This is why we teach our advisors to capture their clients' answers on a Financial Road Map® as described earlier, in chapter 4. The act of writing the answer down in exactly their words demonstrates that you care enough to listen and get it right for them. This is one of the many reasons that a tool like a printed Financial Road Map® is so much more powerful than a yellow pad. The yellow pad demonstrates that the clients' words are only worth capturing on the cheapest piece of paper you have. When you have a compelling visual tool like the Financial Road Map® to capture and present their important words for them, it sends the message that what they say is very important.

While a fact-finder is a step in the right direction, it is really more about the advisor and the financial planning software than it is about the client. Fact-finders were designed to capture information for advisors to use later to do their work, whereas the Financial Road Map® is designed to help put things in perspective for the clients so they can make good choices. It's all about them.

Getting Clear

To give your clients an intelligent and effective course of action, you must first clarify their responses. To *clarify* means "to make transparent, unclouded, distinct, sharp," and "to illuminate." You clarify to get on the same wavelength and to gain a sense of shared meaning. The response you want when you clarify what the other person means is, "Yes, that's it!" or "You've got it!"

Using our methods, the Financial Road Map® helps you clarify simply and accurately. The responses the client has given are right there, and if there is any discrepancy between what clients say and what they mean, it should be immediately apparent. This is why we instruct all advisors, when recording responses, to write the *exact wording* someone gives rather than paraphrasing or rewriting it to sound "better." As we've already established, you will not be able to perfectly understand, so your job is to perfectly capture the precise wording the client gives you. This ensures not only that you were listening in the first place, but also that you have accurate information for the planning stage.

Responding Once You've Listened

Only now is it time to respond. Responding too quickly is a tough, tough habit to break. Attend, acknowledge, clarify, *then* respond. Try it; it works for others, and it will work for you. If you're a skeptic, don't just believe what we're saying. Go out and try it for yourself. You'll never know if you like sushi — or hate it — until you try it.

Responding is the easy part when you've really listened. You can:

- Provide an answer, when it's appropriate
- Redirect the person to someone else or to a useful resource
- Agree to take action
- Suggest options and alternatives

If you can respond in twenty words, don't use fifty. It's better to say too little than to say too much. When you say too little, if other people are interested, they will ask for more. When you say too much, you risk alienating them. As a financial advisor, if you say too much, you're simply wasting their time, an affront few clients are willing to stand for very long.

Remember the 5/55 rule: In a one-hour interview, you should speak for five minutes, and the prospective client should speak or be silent for fifty-five minutes. Even if this sounds like a lofty goal to you, you already know that you talk too much during client meetings, especially the initial interview, don't you? And you know that if you talked less you would be more successful, right? So the two questions are

1. How much too much are you talking?

2. How much more successful would you be if you talked less?

The answers: 1) Way, way too much, and 2) much, much more successful. It's almost impossible to talk too little in the first interview. Remember, it's all about them.

Chapter 6

Put It All Into Action
and Reach Your Next Level
of Success

"Don't wish things were easier;
wish you were better."

~ Jim Rohn

HE TWO-STEP LISTENING FORMULA is the simplest and most effective model for Trusted Advisors.™ *Ask! Listen!* It is a formula for success in the people business. Most salespeople use another formula: *Talk! Talk more!* Don't be a salesperson. Be a Trusted Advisor.™

Listening is how you find out what motivates a person to take action. You can't motivate people. They must motivate themselves. When you light a fire under a snail, you get escargot. But when you light a fire under a person's dreams, you get action. Listen for what motivates them, and then give it to them.

Listening is the most effective road to success for financial advisors. Why? Because relationships with ideal clients are built on trust, and because people implement financial plans for their reasons, not yours. Stop giving them your reasons and listen for theirs instead.

Most of us could spend our lifetimes improving our listening skills — and we should. This is not like tying your shoes; you don't just pick it up in a couple of days then never have to think about it again. Instead, even the best listeners constantly strive for new ways to be more attentive, more insightful, more in tune with other people. We hope this book has shown you how and why listening well and more can powerfully affect your quality of life and that of your clients, family, and friends.

In closing, we'd like to share with you the story of Mark Little, a financial advisor in San Antonio, Texas. Mark was the first client of Bachrach & Associates, Inc. to "be done"[4] with prospecting and marketing. He did it by precisely following all the methods outlined in our programs. That is to say, he listened.

Did it pay off? It did: He has reduced his workweek from six days to three, increased his production from $388,000 to more than $1.4 million a year, and drastically reduced his clientele from 1,242 clients to serve only 100 people whom he sincerely enjoys advising. Did you really absorb that whole sentence? That's a lot to take in: He works half as much, earns more than three times as much, and deals only with people who get it. He did all this during a time (1999 to 2002) when markets declined, world events rocked investor confidence, and most advisors were thrilled

---

4. To learn more about how to finish the prospecting and marketing phase of your business, refer to the *Being Done Special Report* offered by Bachrach & Associates, Inc., consult the resources offered in the back of this book, visit www.BachrachVBS.com, or call (800) 347-3707.

if they kept the bottom from dropping out of their production. Think about that for a moment before you read on.

At first, because he had been doing quite well already and had his own opinions about how to be successful in a financial services practice, he resisted many of the specific instructions and tools the professionals in the Trusted Advisor™ programs are given. But, he has said on numerous occasions and to many of his peers, every time he surrendered and just followed the method, it worked to his advantage. Ultimately, he discovered that listening — *both to the advice he was receiving and, as a result, to his clients* — had both professional and personal rewards beyond what he'd imagined for himself.

We wrote this book to help advisors who use our method get better results. Ultimately, it all rests upon the single skill of listening. Whether you use our interview method and our tools, or something else, the ideas in this book will help you connect with your clients and serve them at an entirely new level of excellence. We wish you great success, both in your professional and in your personal life. When you choose to be a Trusted Advisor™ and not a salesperson, it's easy to remember it's all about them.

ABOUT THE AUTHORS

Bill Bachrach, CSP is a speaker, trainer, and consultant to the financial services industry. He is also the author of the industry bestseller, *Values-Based Selling: The Art of Building High-Trust Client Relationships*. He created the three-day Values-Based Selling™ Academy for financial professionals and managers at all levels, and the one-year Trusted Advisor Coach® program for top producers. His latest book, *Values-Based Financial Planning*, teaches consumers how to align their financial choices with their personal core values and how to make the best decision about doing it themselves or hiring a Trusted Advisor.™

Bill is considered the industry's leading resource for helping financial professionals make the transition from being salespeople to being Trusted Advisors.™ In January of 2001, the readers of *Financial Planning* magazine named Bill Bachrach one of the four most influential people in our business. Values-Based Selling™ is the single most powerful process proven to help financial professionals build high-trust client relationships on purpose. It is widely acknowledged as the *only proven*, transferable method for teaching financial professionals to build high-trust relationships.

On a personal note, in 1998 Bill successfully completed the Hawaii Ironman Triathlon. The 2.4-mile swim, 112-mile bike ride, and 26.2-mile marathon run held annually in hot, windy, rugged volcanic terrain is considered the toughest single-day athletic event in the world.

Steve Shapiro is the author of the bestseller, *Listening for Success*, now published in seven languages. Steve specializes in one-to-one selling: realtors, networkers, insurance, financial planners, et al.

Even months or years after experiencing his message, people report how the quality of their personal and professional relationships have deepened, expanded, and prospered.

His speeches and seminars are in demand around the world. Steve's presentations are known for their immediate transformative affect on listeners — sales increase and relationships at home improve within days. Organizations including American Express, Compaq, Yamaha, Marriott, Safeguard Insurance, National Association of Insurance Women, Nortel, and leading network marketing companies use his audio and video programs, and engage him as a speaker. You must experience his passion to appreciate the power of his message.

Steve is also a competitive athlete, martial artist and adventure traveler, including a 1,000-mile trek of the Amazon river. He got his start in speaking at the age of 19 as a performer in the Birds of Prey Show at the San Diego Wild Animal Park.

About Bachrach & Associates, Inc.

The strategic objective of Bachrach & Associates, Inc. is to transform financial professionals from successful salespeople to mega-successful Trusted Advisors™.

After 15 years of development, implementation, and refinement the results speak for themselves. Financial professionals who implement Bachrach's Values-Based Selling™ and Values-Based Financial Planning™ methods create first interview *experiences* so profound that 5 things *naturally* occur:

1. People hire you to create a written financial plan and pay whatever you ask.

2. They give you all their money and stop working with other advisors.

3. They ignore financial pornography.

4. They do whatever you tell them to do.

5. They introduce you to everyone they know who meets your Ideal Client Profile.

This is not the promise of benefits from cleverly written marketing material. These are the proven facts of what happens for advisors who abandon traditional sales techniques and learn to behave like Trusted Advisors™.

Bachrach & Associates, Inc. has the tools to help individual financial professionals make the transition to being Trusted Advisors™. We also have resources to help financial institutions integrate Values-Based Selling™ into their cultures to bring an entire organization of Trusted Advisors™ to their clients.

8380 Miramar Mall, Suite 200
San Diego, CA 92121
Tel. (800) 347-3707
Fax (858) 558-0748
E-mail: info@BachrachVBS.com
http://www.BachrachVBS.com

Resources from Bachrach & Associates, Inc.

For a fraction of the value of one good client, you will enjoy a lifetime of results from the
Values-Based Selling™ Mastery System!

You Get It All! *for only $599*

- *Values-Based Selling* book
- *Values-Based Selling™* audiotapes or CDs
- Values Conversation™ and Financial Road Map® Video Tapes
- Coaching & Follow-up: 4 Group Quarterly Teleconferences with Bill Bachrach

- Financial Road Maps® (package of 25)
- Financial Road Map® (laminated poster for use with dry erase markers)
- *Values-Based Financial Planning* book

Don't wait . . . Order Today!

Mail us the reply card in the back of this book or call (800) 347-3707 to purchase.

Financial Road Map®
A Vital Tool for Inspiring Your Clients To Action

The value of a compelling visual representation of clients' values, goals and current financial reality cannot be underestimated. Bachrach & Associates, Inc. now offers the **Financial Road Map®** featured in this book in a big (27" x 39") laminated poster for use with erasable markers. It's ideal for client meetings and presentations. PRICE $99.

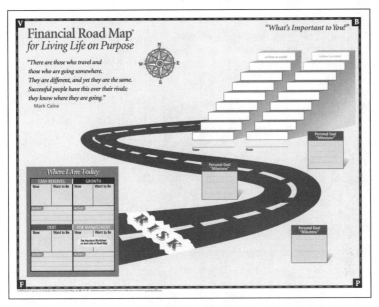

The Financial Road Map® is also available in a 17" x 22" version for desktop use—clients can keep the original and you can keep a copy in your file. The back can be used as a simple fact-finder. PRICE $29 FOR PACKAGE OF 25 MAPS.

Call (800) 347-3707 now for a free sample, or mail us the reply card in the back of this book to purchase.

Success Road Map®
A Vital Tool for Inspiring Existing Producers to Action and for Recruiting

The value of a compelling visual representation of values, goals and current business reality cannot be underestimated.

The **Success Road Map**® is available in a 17" x 22" version for desktop use—producers can keep the original and the leader can keep a copy in the file. The back includes the 9 Core Competencies and planning worksheet, as taught in the *High-Trust Leadership* book.

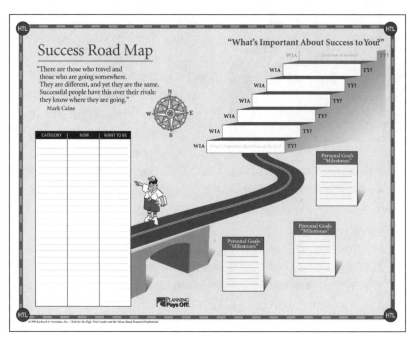

PRICE $29 FOR PACKAGE OF 25 MAPS.

Just like the Financial Road Map® is a vital tool used by advisors with their clients and prospects to inspire them to action, the Success Road Map® creates the same kind of experience with managers/leaders and advisors.

(800) 347-3707   www.bachrachvbs.com

It's All About Them:
How Trusted Advisors Listen For Success
Do You Know What's Important To Your Clients?
Let Listening Be A Key To Your Success.

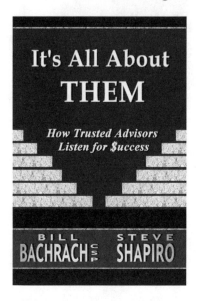

BILL BACHRACH   **STEVE SHAPIRO**

Many financial services professionals are so focused on selling products and services and getting their message across that they forget to listen to what is most important to their clients and prospects.

This book focuses on helping financial services professionals fine tune their listening skills, so that they are listening for success. This book promises greater success with clients, prospects, with your family and spouse too. Listening is the silent skill of success.

Table of Contents:
Introduction: If You Listen to Them, They Will Listen To You
1. Give Clients What They Really Want
2. Know the True Meaning of Listening
3. Pay Attention and Earn Trust
4. Hear the Truth, Tell the Truth, and Get the Truth Every Time
5. Master the Two Steps of Listening for Success and Reap the Rewards
6. Put it All into Action and Reach Your Next Level of Success

Only $14.95 • Volume Discounts Available
Order your copy today!

Call (800) 347-3707 or mail us the reply form
in the back of this section to purchase.

From The Old World to the New World
Audiocassette and Workbook

From The Old World
To The New World

By Bill Bachrach

The purpose of this special tape and script is to demonstrate several conversations you need to master, and conduct frequently, to accelerate "Being Done™". Many Advisors use the "Old World to the New World" strategy to make the transition from commissions to fees.

The most intelligent first step toward Being Done™ is to focus on existing clients. When you create a profound interview experience they will:

1. Hire you to write a plan
2. Give you all of their money and stop working with other advisors.
3. Ignore Financial Pornography.
4. Do what you tell them to do.
5. Introduce you to others who meet your Ideal Client Profile.

And they generate a predictable amount of minimum annual recurring revenue, to be considered an Ideal Client!

Don't be a salesperson. Be a Trusted Advisor™.

*Only $79.00 • Discount Available for
Academy and TAC graduates: $59.00!*
Order your copy today!

*Call (800) 347-3707 or mail us the reply form
in the back of this section to purchase.*

Why Invest Three Days Perfecting Your Client Interview?

The client interview is as much the core skill for financial professionals as the golf swing is for the pro golfer. The client interview is where you build trust, get complete financial disclosure, and get the commitments that **make you money and deliver value to your clients.** It is also where you build the relationships that create a steady flow of referrals so you can **spend less time prospecting and marketing, and more time helping clients.** Of course, the most important aspect of the interview is the quality of the questions and your ability to truly listen. We think listening well is the key to earning peoples' trust.

Practical content you can use immediately to produce results.

You will learn to use the simple, compelling, visual tool called the Financial Road Map® that has helped other advisors like you become million-dollar producers on an accelerated time schedule.

To find out about enrolling in the next Academy session, CALL US at 1-800-347-3707, or VISIT OUR WEBSITE at www.BachrachVBS.com

Tuition includes Academy attendance, breakfast and lunch. Tuition is $2,495 -OR- $1,995 for Values-Based Selling™ Mastery System owners. *(Prices subject to change.)*

(The Values-Based Selling™ Mastery System is the recommended course material.)

**Don't wait. Call today.
(800) 347-3707.**

The Trusted Advisor Coach®

for Successful Financial Professionals Who Seek Perfection in the Client Interview

With the same principles professional athletes use to make small adjustments that produce large performance gains, Bill Bachrach has created a **one-year coaching process** using video tape, intense coaching and feedback.

This program is proven to help very successful financial professionals produce more results in far less time. You will finally discover *exactly* why clients do business with you because, if you are honest with yourself, you probably don't really know.

Isn't it time you did?

To qualify, you must

- show proof of a personal annual income in excess of $100,000,
- be open to frank evaluation of your skills,
- be very good at the client interview right now,
- be familiar with Values-Based Selling™,
- have big goals and a secure ego.

> *"The Trusted Advisor Coach® program has helped me to get laser focused on my ideal clients and develop the skills necessary to get them as clients. In one month alone I have gotten three accounts worth over one million dollars."*
>
> **Keith Cline,** Raymond James & Associates, Inc.

Big goals means income in excess of $250,000, $500,000, $1,000,000 or more. It means two to four months per year of free time. It means a quality of life that includes total goal achievement and values fulfillment. It means truly making a difference in the lives of others.

Because there are few resources and little support in the financial services industry for people who choose to operate at your level, The Trusted Advisor Coach® is a one-year exclusive skill development process designed specifically for you. Using the strategies of elite athletes and interaction with your peers, you will move to a level most financial professionals can't even imagine.

Mail us the reply card in the back of this book or call (800) 347-3707 for further information or to apply today.

Values-Based Financial Planning
*The Next Step in Revolutionizing Your Business—
And the Financial Services Industry*

For the first time ever, the general public has a book to help them understand the unique value of creating a values-based Financial Road Map® and discover how important it is to have a trusted advisor who is a Values-Based Financial Professional™.

As a Trusted Advisor™, you already know that the keys to building your business are the referrals you receive from your most respected clients—and your ability to determine which of those referred people are equipped to appreciate your services and implement the plan you create for them.

You Can:

- purchase quantities of *Values-Based Financial Planning* at a volume discount,
- write a customized introduction to be bound into the front of the books (with a minimum order of 500 copies),
- and give each core client at least five copies to deliver to family and friends who meet your Ideal Client Profile.

Trusted Advisors™ who've implemented this turnkey system – sending clients both the *Values-Based Financial Planning* book and newsletter – tell us they experience both the gratification of a genuine, "value-added" marketing strategy, as well as impressive results with referrals.

***Please call (800) 347-3707 for pricing information
or go to www.bachrachvbs.com***

When You Invest in Our Resources and Programs

We'll support you in producing results–FREE.

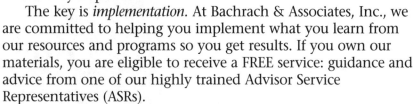

Ever wonder why, with all the great resources available to financial professionals, so few people really use them? Why do only some get the results they hoped for?

The key is *implementation.* At Bachrach & Associates, Inc., we are committed to helping you implement what you learn from our resources and programs so you get results. If you own our materials, you are eligible to receive a FREE service: guidance and advice from one of our highly trained Advisor Service Representatives (ASRs).

Call us now and you will be assigned your own personal ASR who will work with you to maximize your results. That's right: There's no end point, no cutoff or maximum number of times you can speak with your ASR-as long as you are more committed to your success than we are.

We focus on three key steps to assist you with taking your career to the next level:

1. We interview you, having a conversation similar to the one we advise you to have with your clients. You will gain greater clarity about what's important to you, be more committed to your goals, and identify the gaps between where you are now and where you want to be professionally so you increase your probability of reaching your next level.

2. We guide you, giving you concrete actions for making the most of the resource you own or the program you have attended. No more half-read books on your shelf! No more unused audiotapes sitting on your credenza or in the trunk of your car! Instead, get the results you want.

3. We advise you, assessing your situation and recommending next action steps for professional growth and lasting success.

Just call us toll-free at **(800) 347-3707** and request an appointment with an Advisor Service Representative. Or e-mail **info@bachrachvbs.com** with "ASR Appointment Request" in the subject line. Don't leave your untapped potential sitting on the shelf! Make your appointment today.

"Don't be a salesperson. Be a Trusted Advisor™."

(800) 347-3707   www.bachrachvbs.com

The Winning Spirit
A Book of Championship Caliber

"If your profession were an Olympic event, would you make the team?" Bill Bachrach asks this in the first chapter of this extraordinary book of short essays by 20 of the country's finest motivational speakers. Inspired by the determination, spirit and will of Olympic athletes, *The Winning Spirit* considers these same qualities in terms of daily life. In addition to Bill Bachrach's essay, "Olympic Thinking," contributions include

- Jim Tunney on "Mental Biceps,"
- Tony Alessandra on "Take Aim in Life,"
- George Walther on "Win the Gold With Mettle,"
- Bill Brooks on "How to Be Your Own Olympic Coach,"
- Jim Cathcart on "Helping People Grow,"
- Les Brown on "Olympic Dreams."

The Winning Spirit was published in association with the United States Olympic Committee. PRICE $16.95

***Mail us the reply card in the back of this book
or call (800) 347-3707 to purchase.***

BACHRACH & ASSOCIATES, INC. PRODUCT ORDER FORM

ITEM (Volume discounts available on all items—call for details)	QTY	UNIT PRICE	TOTAL
The Mastery System Get it all, and save over $409!		~~$1,008.90~~ **$599.**⁰⁰	
Values Conversation™ Training Video 90 minutes of Values Conversation demonstrations		$159.00	
Financial Road Map® Training Video 2 hours of Financial Road Map demonstrations		$159.00	
Values-Based Selling™ Audio Cassette Series 8+ hours on 8 audio tapes		$199.00	
Values-Based Selling book		$34.95	
Financial Road Map® (22" x 17") Package of 25, paper, for desktop use		$29.00	
Financial Road Map® (39" x 27") Laminated poster; use with dry erase markers		$99.00	
The Values-Based Financial Planning book Customization available: call for details		$29.95	
Teleconference Renewal 4 quarterly calls Available to Mastery System owners only		$299.00	
High-Trust Leadership book		$27.95	
Success Road Map® (22" x 17") Package of 25, paper, for desktop use		$29.00	
The Winning Spirit book Opening chapter by Bill Bachrach, published in association with the U.S. Olympic Committee		$16.95	
Quality of Life Enhancer Worksheets (pad 50)		$19.95	
The Values-Based Financial Planning™ Newsletter		(Call for price)	
Old World to New World booklet & audio		(Call for price)	
It's All About Them (book on listening)		14.95	

(left margin, vertical:) THESE ITEMS ARE INCLUDED IN THE MASTERY SYSTEM

	SUBTOTAL	
	7.75% SALES TAX (California residents only)	
	SHIPPING (See chart)	
	TOTAL $ All funds U.S. dollars	

BACHRACH
 & A S S O C I A T E S • I N C
 Values-Based Selling™

To order call
 (800) 347-3707, <br> visit our website at <br> www.bachrachvbs.com, <br> or photocopy <br> this form and mail to:

Bachrach & Associates, Inc.
 8380 Miramar Mall,
 Suite 200
 San Diego, CA 92121

— or fax to —

(858) 558-0748.

Thank You!

U.S. SHIPPING & HANDLING
(call for charges outside U.S. or to expedite shipping):
Orders are shipped UPS GROUND.

For orders	
up to $50	$ 7.00
$51– $100	$15.00
$101–$300	$20.00
$301–$600	$35.00
Over $600 call for price	

If you desire express delivery, please call us for assistance. International shipping additional. Does not include customs or brokerage fees.

Rev. 9/1/02 • This order form supercedes all previous forms. Prices subject to change.

❏ **Here's my check** (payable to Bachrach & Associates, Inc.).

Please charge my: ❏ American Express ❏ Visa ❏ MasterCard ❏ Discover

Card # _____ Expires _____

Signature _____

Name _____

Company _____

Address _____

City _____ State _____ Zip _____

Phone ( ) _____ Fax ( ) _____

e-mail _____

I'd like to know more! Please call me about
❏ customized keynote speeches or workshops
❏ on-site training and consulting services
❏ customized *Values-Based Financial Planning* books

❏ add me to the content-rich free e-mail
❏ The Values-Based Selling™ Academy
❏ The Trusted Advisor Coach® program for top producers

Listening Resources from Steve Shapiro Listening Systems

Mental Muscle: 7 Principles For Strengthening Your Sales (*6-cassette album*) ~ **$99.00**

25 years of sales research, consulting and field experience went into designing this program. This is the essence of sales success condensed into 3 hours of engaging studio and live recording. You will learn the psychology of why people buy. The message is unique and powerful and if you listen in your car, you will increase your sales.

Steve Shapiro Live (*CD*) ~ **$19.95**

Steve Shapiro weaves stories and principles into a message for you, your business and your family. Recorded live, in front of 400 people, you will receive the same message that makes the audience laugh, cry, and learn. These principles save marriages, transform families, help leaders lead, and show salespeople the truth about selling better.

Listening For Success (*book*) ~ **$9.95**

This best-selling book is now in 7 languages. You can read it in less than an hour, and that hour will change your life and the way you communicate with everyone. Find out why companies buy 20,000 or more at a time and why people buy it for their family and friends. Read it yourself first, before you give it to someone and say, "You need this!"

Miracle of Listening (*2-cassettes*) ~ **$29.95**

In this tape series, international speaker and author Bob Proctor interviews Steve Shapiro on the philosophy of the listening life. Why listen? What is listening? What to listen for. Listening as a path to enlightenment, and much more.

Listening for Success (*video*) ~ **$39.95**

Steve Shapiro lays out the 5 fundamental principles of listening and how to apply them to your business and personal life. In his humorous and hard hitting style, you will want to watch this video with family, friends and co-workers. Share it with your team at work, with salespeople. The principles apply to every area of your life. Low-quality relationships — low quality of life. High quality relationships — high quality of life.

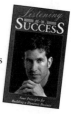

To order call **800-4432-9935** *or go to* **www.steveshapiro.com**